Becoming a
Zombie

by Ruth Owen

Consultant: Luke W. Boyd
Editor in Chief
Zombie Research Society
Los Angeles, California

BEARPORT
PUBLISHING

New York, New York

Credits

Cover, © tsuneomp/Shutterstock and © Crystal Light/Shutterstock; 2–3, © froe_mic/Shutterstock; 4–5, © Kim Jones; 6B, © Volker Steger/Science Photo Library; 6–7, © SvedOliver/Shutterstock; 7, © Kiselev Andrey Valerevich/Shutterstock; 8L, © Victoria Antonova/Shutterstock; 8R, © Anukool Manoton/Shutterstock; 9, © Kateryna Kon/Shutterstock; 10, © Alexilusmedical/Shutterstock; 10R, © Evan Oto/Science Photo Library; 11, © Garo/Phanie/Science Photo Library; 12, © Mireille Vautier/Alamy; 13T, © Beth Swanson/Shutterstock; 13B, © Swapan Photography/Shutterstock; 14–15, © Science Photo Library; 15C, © 18percentgrey/Shutterstock; 16B, © Christian Darkin/Science Photo Library; 16–17, © Kim Jones; 18–19, © Dr. Morley Read/Science Photo Library; 19B, © Jason Bazzano/Alamy; 20TR, Public Domain; 20B, © Dr. Barry Slaven/Science Photo Library; 21TL, © Image Quest Marine/Alamy; 21BL, Dr. Myron G. Schultz/Public Domain; 21R, © Nomad_Soul/Shutterstock; 22TL, © spline_x/Shutterstock; 22BL, © addkm/Shutterstock; 22CT, © Vincent Noel/Shutterstock; 22CB, © junyanjiang/Shutterstock; 22R, © ale de sun/Shutterstock; 23, © Callahan/Shutterstock.

Publisher: Kenn Goin
Senior Editor: Joyce Tavolacci
Creative Director: Spencer Brinker
Photo Researcher: Ruth Owen Books

Library of Congress Cataloging-in-Publication Data

Names: Owen, Ruth, 1967– author.
Title: Becoming a zombie / by Ruth Owen.
Description: New York : Bearport Publishing Company, Inc., 2018. I Series: Zombie zone I
   Includes bibliographical references and index.
Identifiers: LCCN 2017047850 (print) I LCCN 2017049941 (ebook) I
ISBN 9781684024995 (ebook) I ISBN 9781684024414 (library)
Subjects: LCSH: Zombies—Juvenile literature. Classification: LCC GR581 (ebook) I
   LCC GR581.0937 2018 (print) I DDC 398.21—dc23
LC record available at https://lccn.loc.gov/2017047850

For more information, write to Bearport Publishing Company, Inc., 45 West 21st Street, Suite 3B, New York, New York 10010. Printed in the United States of America.

10 9 8 7 6 5 4 3 2 1

Contents

Back from Death

It's late at night in the city **morgue**. In the center of a brightly lit room, a man's dead body is laid out on a metal table. A doctor holding a **scalpel** is performing an **autopsy**. As she slices into the chest of the **corpse**, its icy, gray hand suddenly jerks and then grabs her arm. Snarling, the corpse rises into a sitting position. Then it attacks, biting the woman again and again, until she crumples to the floor and dies.

Within minutes, the doctor's closed eyes flicker open. Her body is covered with gaping, bloody wounds, but she still staggers to her feet. Together, the two zombies shuffle from the morgue. They have returned from the dead . . . and are **ravenous** for human flesh!

The term *zombie* may come from the words *ndzumbi* and *nzambi*, which originate from two African languages. *Ndzumbi* means "corpse" and *nzambi* means "spirit of a dead person."

The Undead

What are zombies exactly? These nightmarish creatures are driven by one desire—to feed on human flesh. Once a zombie bites a person, the victim dies and then becomes a zombie.

A zombie cannot feel pain and keeps on moving even when its body is badly damaged. According to zombie **lore**, the only way to stop the ferocious creature is to destroy its brain.

For now, the flesh-eating undead only exist in books, games, movies, and TV shows. However, what if our worst nightmares were to come true? Could people actually become real-life zombies?

Even though a zombie can move around, its body **decomposes** over time. Its stinking, decaying flesh soon becomes food for hungry **maggots**. Its rotting skin and muscles peel away from its bones, and its hands, arms, or legs may fall off!

Flesh

Maggots

A Zombie Virus?

Viruses cause many horrible diseases. Could a virus mutate, or change, and transform people into zombies?

Rabies is a deadly disease caused by a virus. Most people who get rabies are infected by a bite from a dog or a wild animal that has the disease. Once infected, the person becomes confused and aggressive. He or she may froth at the mouth and have difficulty walking and talking.

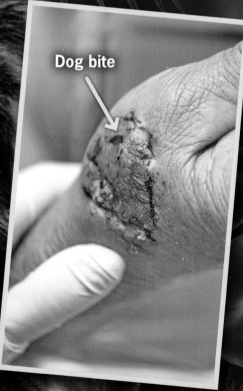

Dog bite

If the rabies virus were to mutate, could it also cause its human victims to attack and bite other people—just like zombies? For now, scientists don't think this will happen. However, it's a fact that viruses can change. For example, flu viruses that affect animals such as pigs and birds often mutate. Once this happens, the viruses can be deadly to humans.

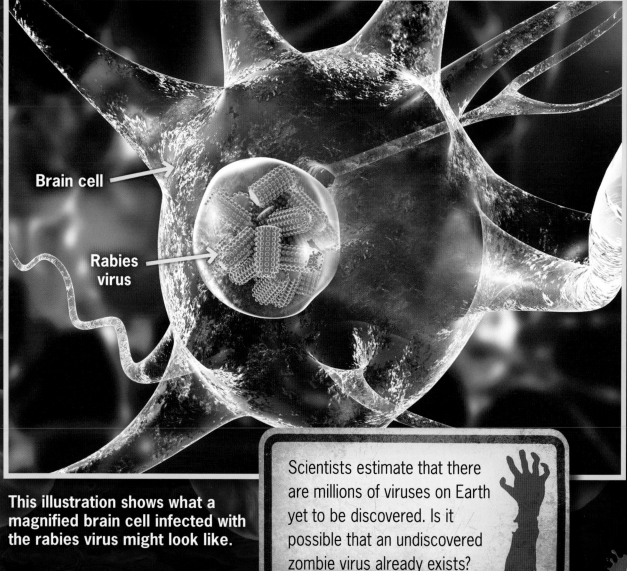

Brain cell

Rabies virus

This illustration shows what a magnified brain cell infected with the rabies virus might look like.

Scientists estimate that there are millions of viruses on Earth yet to be discovered. Is it possible that an undiscovered zombie virus already exists?

Brain Invaders

Could something other than a virus attack a person's brain and turn him or her into a zombie? One possibility is an infection caused by something called a prion.

A person's body contains extremely tiny particles called proteins. Sometimes misshapen proteins called prions infect a person's brain. Then the prions cause normal proteins in the brain to change shape, too.

A healthy protein

A misshapen prion

As more and more proteins change shape, a person's brain cells either become damaged or die. One example of a terrible disease caused by prions is Creutzfeldt-Jakob disease (CJD).

Prions cause holes to form in a victim's brain, turning it into spongy material. As the brain becomes badly damaged, parts of it shut down. Then the victim might be unable to talk. The invading prions could put the person in a zombielike state!

A slice of human brain being examined by a scientist for a prion disease

In some parts of the United States, deer, elk, and moose are suffering from a condition called Chronic Wasting Disease (CWD). This disease is caused by prions. The animals have blank eyes and drooping heads, and they stagger and stumble—much like zombies!

11

Zombie Poison

On the Caribbean island of Haiti, zombies are thought to be very real. It's believed that **witch doctors** called **bokors** have been turning people into the living dead for hundreds of years!

According to Haitian tales, a bokor might poison a person using a homemade potion. After the victim dies and is buried, the bokor digs up the corpse and uses magic to bring it back to life as a zombie.

The bokor then controls the zombie and uses the creature as a slave by feeding it a fruit called zombie cucumber.

This painting from Haiti shows a bokor controlling two zombie slaves.

Could there be any truth to this story? Some scientists think the potion made by bokors contains a deadly poison that comes from puffer fish. The poison paralyzes the victim, making the person appear to be dead. However, once the poison's effects wear off, the victim miraculously appears to have been brought back to life.

Puffer fish

Zombie cucumber, or datura, is a highly poisonous plant. If a person were to eat its fruit, he or she might become very confused and begin to act like a zombie.

Datura fruit

Creating a Zombie Brain

Can Haitian witch doctors really bring the dead back to life? No one can say for sure. In the future, however, medical doctors hope to raise the dead—but how?

Sometimes, a person's brain can become injured in an accident or damaged by disease. The person's brain may then die, but his or her body remains unharmed and can be kept alive using machines. Could the person's brain ever be repaired?

Human brain

Doctors are looking into ways to bring a dead brain back to life using **stem cells**. When injected, these special cells can help a person's body repair itself. The hope is that stem cells can be used in the future to grow new brain tissue and help heal a damaged brain.

However, what if only certain parts of the brain came back to life? Would the person come back as a zombie?

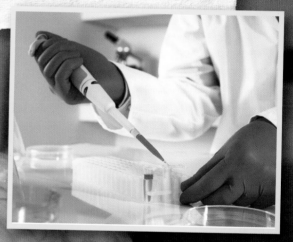

A scientist carrying out stem cell research

Could a human brain be zombified in some other way? In the 1968 movie *Night of the Living Dead*, people were turned into zombies by **radiation** that came from outer space. Might radiation kill off a person's brain cells, leaving him or her just enough brainpower to act like a zombie?

Beware of Robots!

Imagine a zombie with a robot-controlled brain. Not possible? Think again. This terrifying idea could one day become reality.

In the future, tiny robots, called nanorobots, might be injected into the human body. These microscopic robots would be so small that hundreds, or perhaps thousands, could fit on a single grain of rice!

Nanorobots could be used to treat illnesses, for example, by carrying drugs directly to diseased cells. Nanorobots might one day be able to repair a person's damaged brain. However, could they also be used to control the human brain—and turn a person into a bloodthirsty zombie?

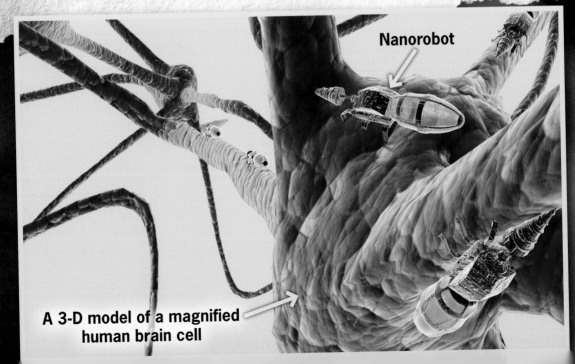

Nanorobot

A 3-D model of a magnified human brain cell

Nanorobots may be able to replicate, or make copies of themselves, inside a person's body. Then the robots could spread from person to person by directing their zombie **hosts** to bite people. After a bite, a swarm of nanorobots might stream from the zombie's mouth into a new host.

Zombie Insects

In the jungles of Brazil, zombification is already happening. Here, a type of **fungus** exists that turns ants into zombies!

Fungi **reproduce** by spreading tiny seedlike parts called spores. The spores of the zombie fungus infect an ant's body with substances that make it unable to function normally. Once zombified, the ant does only what the fungus needs it to do!

Ball of spores

Ant corpse

The ant attaches itself to a plant on the forest floor and holds on tight. Slowly, the fungus kills the ant and uses its tiny corpse as its new home. Eventually, a ball filled with new spores sprouts from the ant's head and body. Then the ball bursts, spreading new spores into the jungle!

Ball of spores growing out of ant's head

Other bugs have also been turned into zombies. The Costa Rican **parasitoid** wasp lays its egg on a spider. A larva hatches from the egg and injects a chemical into the spider that turns it into a zombielike slave. Then the zombie spider builds a special web for the larva, where the young wasp can live as it changes into an adult.

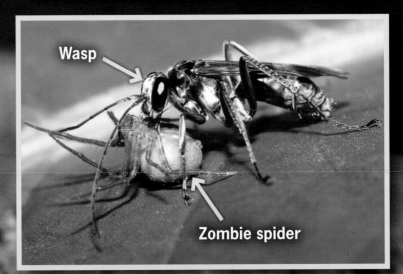

Wasp

Zombie spider

Real-Life Zombie Diseases

Some real-life diseases have similar symptoms to zombification. A horrifying infection called leprosy, or Hansen's disease, causes a person's skin to form sores and lumps. Over time, people can lose feeling in their fingers and toes. After infection sets in, a victim's fingers, toes, or even his or her nose can become badly misshapen. Sometimes, infected body parts may have to be cut off!

Tissue necrosis

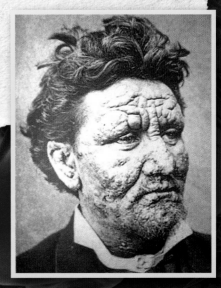

A man with leprosy in the 1800s

A condition called tissue necrosis causes a person's flesh to turn black, die, and then rot—even though the person is still alive.

In Africa, thousands of people suffer from a disease called sleeping sickness, which is spread by tsetse flies. A fly bites a person and injects microscopic, wormlike **parasites** into his or her body. Once the parasites invade the victim's brain, he or she may have trouble walking and talking. The infected person may be sleepy in the day and awake at night—just like a zombie in a horror movie.

Tsetse fly biting a person

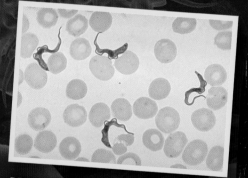

Magnified sleeping sickness parasites in human blood

Perform a Zombie Autopsy

If a zombie virus ever breaks out, scientists may have to examine the bodies of destroyed zombies to learn more about them. Do you and your friends have the "guts" to perform a zombie autopsy?

You will need:

- 5 shoe boxes with lids
- Scissors
- 5 bowls
- A marker or pen
- Paper
- 5 foods to use as zombie body parts (see examples at right)

Brain
(cauliflower)

Pieces of skin
(beef jerky)

Veins
(cold cooked spaghetti)

Heart
(lump of red jello)

Eyeballs
(peeled grapes)

Get Ready to Play:

1. One person is the game leader. He or she should carefully cut a hole in the lid of each shoe box that's large enough to fit a person's hand. Then number the boxes 1 to 5.

2. Place one zombie body part (food item) in a bowl inside each box far enough away from the hole. Don't show the other players the food items being used.

How to Play:

1. Taking turns, the other players must put their hands inside each box and touch the body part.

2. The player must guess the zombie body part and write down the answer. For an extra point, the player can also guess the food item.

3. The player with the most points wins!

Glossary

autopsy (AW-top-see) a detailed examination of a dead body

bokors (BOH-kurz) voodoo priests or sorcerers who are believed to use supernatural powers for evil purposes

corpse (KORPS) a dead body

decomposes (dee-kuhm-POHS-iz) rots and falls apart

fungus (FUHN-guhss) a plantlike living thing, such as a mushroom

hosts (HOHSTZ) living things, such as people or animals, that become the home of another living thing

lore (LAWR) traditional beliefs and stories

maggots (MAG-uhts) the wormlike young of flies, which often feed on dead bodies

morgue (MORG) a place where dead bodies are kept before burial

parasites (PA-ruh-sites) living things that make their home on or inside another living thing

parasitoid (PAR-uh-si-toid) using another living thing as food, a home, or a place to raise young

radiation (ray-dee-AY-shuhn) a form of energy that can be very dangerous to living things

ravenous (RAV-uh-nuhss) extremely hungry

reproduce (ree-pruh-DOOSS) to produce more of the same thing

scalpel (SKAL-puhl) a very sharp, straight knife

stem cells (STEM SELZ) cells that can develop into many other types of cells

viruses (VYE-ruhss-iz) microscopic organisms that infect cells and cause disease

witch doctors (WICH dok-turz) priests, magicians, or other people with special powers

BEWARE
OF
ZOMBIES

Index

Read More

Axelrod-Contrada, Joan. *Body-Snatchers: Flies, Wasps, and Other Creepy Crawly Zombie Makers (Real-Life Zombies)*. North Mankato, MN: Capstone (2016).

Johnson, Rebecca L. *Zombie Makers: True Stories of Nature's Undead*. Minneapolis, MN: Lerner (2012).

Kamberg, Mary-Lane. *Investigating Zombies and the Living Dead (Understanding the Paranormal)*. New York: Rosen (2015).

Learn More Online

To learn more about becoming a zombie, visit
www.bearportpublishing.com/ZombieZone

About the Author

Ruth Owen has been developing and writing children's books for more than 10 years. She lives in Cornwall, England, just minutes from the ocean. If there's a zombie apocalypse, she intends to escape by boat!